T0362887

KOKODA
The Fight for Australia
Sharlene G. Coombs

KNOWLEDGE
BOOKS AND SOFTWARE

8

Teacher Notes:

This recount of the story of the battle of Kokoda in Papua New Guinea is one of Australia's most important war stories and the closest to home. It details how close the Japanese came to invading Australia and reveals the incredible bravery, hardships and mateship of our Aussie Diggers as they stuggled to defend their country from a fierce, and highly disciplined Japanese fighting force. The teamwork, courage and persistence of the Aussies is something that should never be forgotten.

Discussion points for consideration:

1. Discuss the reasons why Japan decided to invade Australia. What were they trying to achieve by doing this?

2. What do you think it would have been like growing up in Japan at this time? How have things changed now?

3. The Japanese had many advantages over the Australians. Discuss these further.

4. Despite these advantages, the Aussie Diggers defeated the Japanese. Why?

Sight words, difficult to decode words, and infrequent words to be introduced and practised before reading this book:

Yamamoto, stronger, smashed, important, resources, controlling, Indonesia, Admiral, camouflage, experience, revenge, dysentery, struggling, commented, conditions, emotional, northern, American, Australian, victories, traditional, samurai, attitude, military, infections, battalion, casualties, emerging.

Acknowledgement of the First Nations' People: We acknowledge the Traditional Owners of country throughout Australia and recognise their continuing connection to land, waters and culture. We pay our respects n, kilometres, rescue, information, understanding.

Contents

1. About Japan's Plan

In the early 1900's, Japan was growing stronger every year. It had become a powerful modern country. It had a war with Russia. Japan destroyed Russia's navy at a Chinese port. It was the first time Japan had won against Europe. This victory gave Japan a feeling of power, that they could beat anyone.

However, Japan lacked something important: the materials to make weapons. These were iron ore, coal and oil. These are called natural resources. Japan's leaders wanted to control all of Asia and the Pacific. But to do so, they needed these resources.

3

By 1940, Japan was controlling most of Asia. Korea was controlled by Japan. Japan was at war with China. It had control of the oil fields in Indonesia and the rubber areas of Malaysia.

The Japanese now set their sights on Australia. The Japanese soldiers were given Australian invasion money. This was money to use when they got to Australia.

The Japanese were ready to go to war with Australia. After the attack on Pearl Harbor in December 1941, Japanese Admiral Yamamoto now wanted to attack Australia.

Australia is a big country. To attack the command areas, Japan had to have airbases. It was too far to fly from Timor. The Japanese planned to hop down the coast of Queensland. This would mean capturing airfields so they could use planes.

To get to Australia, they needed a place that was close enough so that they could attack from the air and by sea. Papua New Guinea was the perfect spot just off the northern coastline of Australia. If the Japanese could invade it and build airfields, they could bomb Australia's coast with their planes and their ships.

2. Battle of the Coral Sea

Papua New Guinea was defended by soldiers at Port Moresby in the south. Port Moresby was important.

The Japanese sent their navy around Papua New Guinea to attack Port Moresby by air and sea. The Japanese navy met the American and Australian navy ships. Both sides attacked each other with fighter and torpedo planes. A lot of the battleships were lost. It was a loss by both sides, but it was the first time the Japanese had been turned back. This was called the Battle of the Coral Sea.

It stopped the Japanese reaching Port Moresby. They now needed to come overland.

3. Battle of Midway

A month later, the Japanese navy was attacked again and lost most of their ships. This was the biggest victory of the Pacific war. The first bombing raids had now started attacking Japan itself. It was the start of pushing the Japanese back.

The Japanese were not running away, and carried on with their plans to get to Port Moresby. They decided the best way to get there was to go across the country. They thought there was a road they could use. It was not a road but a muddy track. The track went over the rugged and very steep Owen Stanley Ranges. It also passed through a tiny village in the highlands called Kokoda, which had an airstrip.

4. The Village of Kokoda

Kokoda's airstrip was vital for the Australians and the Japanese. This would be valuable for dropping food and ammo to keep their soldiers going. Once the Japanese soldiers reached Port Moresby via the Kokoda Track, they could send their warships around to attack from the sea. Port Moresby could then be used as a base to attack Australia.

5. The Japanese Army

The Japanese armies were skillful. They had been fighting in China too! Traditional Japanese warriors were called samurai. They believed that they would become a higher spirit if they died on the battlefield.

This attitude was also drilled into the Japanese army from when they were kids. In school, they had to practise skills like marching, shooting, and hand-to-hand combat. After school, all males went into the military for a part of their lives. It was their duty to fight for their country and their Emperor. The rules were harsh, and they were often beaten by their officers.

The Japanese also had jungle training and weapons that were designed for the climate. Their jungle camouflage was also excellent, making them very hard to spot. In comparison, the Aussies had uniforms that were designed for the desert rather than the jungle. This made it easy for the Japanese to see them. Most of the Aussie weapons were old and had been used during WW1. They didn't work very well in the wet and humid conditions.

The Japanese soldiers carried over 50kg of supplies. They carried their own food and ammo. They landed on the north coast and marched inland to the mountains.

6. The Fight Back Begins

The Japanese plan was found out by the Australian Government. They knew they had to send Australian soldiers to Port Moresby. However, there was a big problem. Australia had almost all of their troops in Europe and the Middle East fighting Germany. There were not enough trained men left to defend Australia against Japanese attacks.

Australian men started joining the Citizens Military Forces, the "militia." Here, they practised shooting and marching. Most of these soldiers had limited experience and training. Some were only 16 years old and had lied about their age.

Word was coming through about the terrible treatment of Australian prisoners of war. The Japanese were showing incredible cruelty. Men were being starved and beaten to death. Captured pilots were killed and not taken as prisoners.

The war in China was horrific. The Japanese had used poisons to kill tens of thousands of innocent people.

In the Philippines, little children had been stabbed with bayonets and left to die on the streets. The war was turning and the view towards the Japanese was one of deadly revenge.

7. The "Chocolate" Soldiers

The Australian Imperial Force (AIF) soldiers called the militia "chocos" or "chocolate soldiers" as they reckoned they would melt when the fighting heated up. This bunch of Aussies became known as the 39th Battalion and they all had one thing in common - their desire to protect their country against all odds. Victoria's 39th and NSW's 53rd Battalions became the first Australian soldiers to land at Port Moresby to help defend their country.

The Aussie soldiers spent six days at sea watching fish swimming past their portholes in the heavily overloaded ship. For some, it was like an adventure. They had never been on a ship before. Others imagined they were going to a palm-fringed island with beautiful beaches and coconut palms dotted along the shore.

They arrived at Port Moresby to find it hot, humid, very smelly, and full of mosquitoes. In the distance they could also see the high peaks of the Owen Stanley Range. This is where they would be fighting before too long.

The heat, humidity, rain, and mosquitoes nearly drove them mad. But the bigger problems were malaria from the mozzies and dysentery from the gross filth.

Many of them were sick within the first few weeks but they still had to unload ships, and build roads and air-raid shelters. They all lost about 10kg in the first few weeks. After 9 weeks on the track, some had lost more than 30kg and were just skin and bones.

They had dysentery and had cut holes in the back of their pants so they could quickly go to the toilet.

8. The Kokoda Battle

The day after Australian troops landed in Port Moresby, the Japanese air force bombed Rabaul in the north. They then used the airfields at Rabaul to attack Port Moresby where the Australian soldiers were based.

On 19 February 1942, the Japanese bombed Darwin. They sank eight ships, destroyed many planes and buildings and killed 243 Australians. Japanese bombing continued in Port Moresby for several months while the soldiers were busy "digging in".

28

The original Japanese plan to take Port Moresby failed. On 20th of July, the Japanese commenced plan B. Their ships landed at Buna in the north. Thousands of tons of supplies, weapons and ammunition were unloaded along with 25,000 troops. If they couldn't take Port Moresby by sea, they would take it inland by the Kokoda Track.

While this was happening up north, the 39th Battalion had been struggling up the track towards Kokoda. The aim was to get there before the Japanese and secure the airfield for supply drops. They did it tough. Many people have commented that the conditions at Kokoda were even worse than those in Gallipoli.

They struggled up near-vertical mountains with heavy packs, rifles, and ammo. The tropical rains quickly made the track muddy and slippery. Blisters became a big problem, along with infections from insect bites. Clothes, shoes and packs were wet most of the time and food supplies were scarce.

Kokoda village was secured by the Australians but not for long. On the 29th of July, Japanese soldiers came in from the other side.The Aussies had to go back down the track. Going back became a pattern for the Australians to save their soldiers. Each time they were pushed back, they would dig new holes ready to fight again.

The Japanese did front-on charges and were smashed by the dug-in Australian soldiers. It meant the Japanese had to lose a lot of soldiers to get ahead. Each time the Australians would regroup, dig-in, and get ready for the next attack. They did this all along the track. They were not holding the Japanese but destroying them.

After Kokoda fell, the Australian 7th Division soldiers who had fought in the Middle East were brought in. Along with these new soldiers, the native porters had a new role. They carried out the injured soldiers and became known affectionately as the "Fuzzy Wuzzy Angels". They were indeed angels and lifesavers, and very brave ones too!

The battle between the Japanese and the Australians was fought in the jungle. Aussie signals soldiers were used for aiming the artillery. The bombs would land just in front of them, and they would signal back to the artillery to re-aim their shots. The signals soldiers were so close, they could hear the Japanese whispering.

Machine gunners would stick their head above the long grass. They would get a position and then fire. The Japanese were only 100 metres in front of them.

They had bayonets fixed on their rifles. The Japanese sometimes charged their positions and used bayonets rather than bullets.

After weeks of fighting and retreat, the Japanese had almost made it to their goal of Port Moresby. The Japanese could see Port Moresby. However, they had lost thousands of soldiers on the way. They were also much further away from their supplies. Ammo supplies were low, and they had very little food left.

For the Aussies, however, things were finally looking up. They were much closer to their supplies and to fresh soldiers to help them out. They also finally had the firepower they needed to make a difference. The remaining Japanese soldiers were being killed quickly and were soon given the order to retreat to Buna.

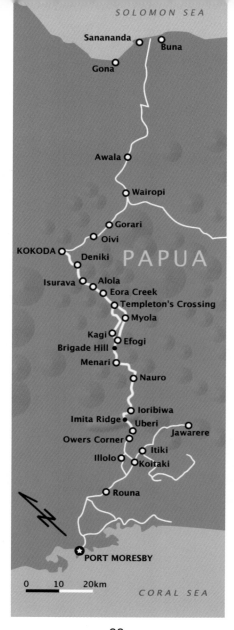

SOLOMON SEA

Sanananda
Buna
Gona

Awala

Wairopi

Gorari
Oivi
KOKODA
Deniki
Isurava
Alola
Eora Creek
Templeton's Crossing
Myola
Kagi
Brigade Hill
Efogi
Menari
Nauro

Ioribiwa
Imita Ridge
Uberi
Jawarere
Owers Corner
Itiki
Illolo
Koitaki

Rouna

PAPUA

PORT MORESBY

0   10   20km

CORAL SEA

38

The Australians chased them all the way there and then joined with the Americans to destroy their base at Buna and Gona.

As the Aussie Diggers walked away from the final battlefield, most of them had been in battle for six months. Over this period, 2,165 Australians had been killed, and 3,533 had been wounded. In comparison, it is estimated that 13,000 Japanese soldiers were killed and many more wounded. Our Aussie soldiers had suffered hugely in so many ways. They had physical and emotional scars and horrible memories that would haunt them forever. But they had smashed a large army. They did this by being free people who were smarter than the enemy at warfare.

These words of remembrance tell us all we want to know: *"They shall grow not old, as we that are left grow old. Age shall not weary them, nor the years condemn. At the going down of the sun, and in the morning, we shall remember them."*

These days, we continue to remember the incredible efforts, bravery, and sacrifices that our soldiers made at Kokoda through our Anzac Day ceremonies. However, the younger people are also getting more involved in a different way. Many are paying tribute to our Kokoda soldiers by walking the Kokoda Track.

9. Kokoda Legacy

Australia was now safe once again. That was something worth fighting for.

In 1992, Paul Keating was the first Australian Prime Minister to visit Kokoda. Flying over the track and looking down over the Owen Stanley Ranges, the PM was clearly upset. Upon emerging from the chopper, he fell to his knees and kissed the ground. It was a symbol of the fact that Australia was finally recognising what had been achieved in this place. Soldiers died in defence of Australia. It is important to remember the high values shown by the brave Australians on this muddy track. These battles stopped the invasion of Australia.

Word Bank

Yamamoto	conditions	military
stronger	emotional	slippery
smashed	straight	infections
important	northern	battalion
resources	American	casualties
controlling	Australian	emerging
Indonesia	reaching	
Admiral	victories	
camouflage	highlands	
experience	important	
revenge	traditional	
dysentery	samurai	
struggling	attitude	
commented	marching	